Reminiscence

by Alvin Randall Enlow

TURNER PUBLISHING COMPANY
Publishers of America's History

Turner Publishing Company Staff
Editors: Dayna Spear/Levi Burkett
Designer: Tyranny J. Bean

Copyright © 2001 Al Enlow.
All rights reserved.
Publishing Rights:
Turner Publishing Company

Library of Congress
Control No: 2001098725
ISBN 978-1-68162-305-4

TABLE OF
CONTENTS

DEDICATION

This narrative is dedicated to the two true loves of my life: first, in memory of Marilyn-Jean, my beloved wife and companion of nearly 48 years. Then, in remembrance of Myfanwy and those too few moments together so long ago.

INTRODUCTION

As a veteran of 24 months overseas service at an 8th Air Force Base in England during World War II, I had always looked forward to a return visit to that ancestral land I had found so welcoming and so interesting.

In the Spring of 1982 my wife and I reached the United Kingdom as part of a European vacation. After sight-seeing in London we rented a small stick shift car and started on our way, to us, on the wrong side of the road.

Following a self-directed circle tour which included Portsmouth (home of Nelson's flagship HMS Victory), the old Roman town of Bath, Shakespeare's Stratford-On-Avon, we headed for Norfolk, hoping to find the old air base and any related nostalgia.

Movie goers may recall the beginning of the great film, *Twelve O'clock High*, wherein the former adjutant takes a bike and pedals out to the old air field and the flashback story ensues.

Heading east from King's Lynn towards Norwich we came to the almost nonexistent village and the old wartime neighborhood. Stopping at the local pub, I asked directions of the proprietor.

Informed that, yes, there was an air base somewhere. "Try that little road across the way." (Or words to that effect.) I still hoped to find something remembered.

Having found no familiar landmark, we finally met a small lorry and the driver gave us more explicit advice and told us that no buildings remained. Even the old Control Tower had recently been torn down.

We did locate the perimeter strip and then, the main runway, to find a large turkey barn right in the middle and a crop dusting plane landing on the strip. The former duck pond where our enlisted control tower crew had often found edible eggs also was nonexistent. (Nostalgia, where are you?)

All that remains of that not-to-be forgotten site is a neatly maintained memorial to all the squadrons and units stationed there, decades ago.

So, half a century later, I felt a need to recall some of the incidents of those not quite forgotten years, humorous and otherwise. Perhaps it is merely a personal catharsis but, hopefully, there may be material of some interest to others.

What follows is intended as reminiscence, not history. Many outstanding books and articles have been written through the years about the many groups and other units of the Mighty 8th Air Force including the 392nd and the 44th Bomb Groups.

I have referred to letters sent home, a diary and to memory. The latter was certainly the most fallible.

As years went by I lost touch with most old Army friends. I will accept my share of the blame for correspondence never sent or answered. One exception is a Control Tower comrade in Houston, TX. We still exchange Christmas cards and notes most every year.

Should anyone I once knew ever read this rambling narrative, please write and I will answer.

CHAPTER 1

Except for one British-born member of our outfit, few, if any of the enlisted men in our squadron had ever been over-seas; so, when our ship finally docked at Swansea, Wales, we were all curious to see how a really foreign country would appear. After all, our only knowledge of such places would have come from books and probably, more likely, from the movies.

Among the sights that caught my eye after disembarking from the ship in Swansea were signs for "COCA-COLA" and a Woolworth's "3 and 6 pence" store. Foreign country?

A far more startling sight as our train reached the London area, were the extensive bombed ruins of homes and other buildings, a stark reminder that we were, indeed, entering a war zone, in obvious comparison with the safety of the country we had just left. Actually seeing these horrid relics of the London blitz in person rather than in a newsreel or magazine at home was a shocking reality.

On a happier note, in contrast to these marks of war, I'm sure none of our group lost any time in noticing the many pretty

Bomb ruins of homes, East Anglia

British girls, easily visible from the train cars and later, from the Army trucks. More about that major subject, later.

Getting used to the total blackout when night fell took some doing upon reaching our previously unknown air base destination. No lights were permitted! Even lighting a cigarette outside in the open was frowned upon. Vehicle headlights were mere slits. Every entrance, doorway and of course, all windows, were covered completely by heavy drapes or other means. This was the case everywhere. On totally clouded over nights, it was all but impossible to see your hand in front of your own face; again, a constant reminder that Great Britain and all her people (and now, ourselves) were totally involved in this long war.

Much later on in Norwich, I remember bumping hard into an apparent local civilian one very dark night. Neither of us had been aware of the other as we groped along, touching the buildings with hands for navigational assistance.

"Watch where you're going, Yank!" came the quick shout. (I could never figure out how the man knew I wasn't English?)

On another occasion, I had arranged to meet a close friend from home, also a GI, in the historic town of Bath. After winter darkness fell, we headed down a steep hill, on foot, to reach a particular restaurant. Suddenly, as we walked and talked, I realized I was alone.

Soundlessly, in the total blackness, without any warning, my friend had fallen down the open steps leading to a below ground level flat!

Nothing broken, merely surprised and bruised, we continued but, one much more careful step at a time until we safely reached our intended destination.

One Autumn, rumors abounded concerning German paratroopers being dropped near East Anglian Air Bases to disrupt operational activities. Most of us scoffed at these "warnings."

But the mind and imagination can often enlarge rumors beyond their logical reason. My own imagination in this instance was an example of such exaggeration.

On a bright moonlit October night, I left the cozy barracks aboard my creaking bicycle to report for duty at the Control

B-24 No. 268, 576th Squadron, Wendling

Tower at midnight. As I pedaled my lonely way down the empty road toward the airfield, a heavy ground fog, contrasting with the clear, full moonlight, created an increasingly frightening landscape. Imagination then took over and the previously laughed at thought of German soldiers hiding behind trees, haystacks and hedgerows became spookily more real the further and faster I rode.

Shivering with imagined thoughts of enemies hidden along the road, I pedaled even faster and more furiously; foolishly but thoroughly spooked until I neared the Control Tower. I seem to remember abandoning my bike in full flight and breathlessly bounding up the tower steps perhaps three at a time?

When daylight replaced brilliant moonlight I discovered my deserted bike about 50 feet from the door to Flying Control, undoubted evidence that I had, indeed, succumbed to that chilling, self-induced fright.

No news ever did reach us of any real life Germans having dropped in for an unwelcome visit, then or later.

As at most American Air Corps bases, our B-24 Liberators were often decorated by skilled and imaginative crew chiefs or other artists, with pictures of sexy damsels and other fitting illustrations. On one of our bombers, the artist had cleverly managed to position the pictured bouncing, busty beauty to exactly fit protruding rivets in the appropriate locations.

One unfortunate accident on the air base involved a taxiing airplane overtaking a civilian British lorry on the perimeter strip. A propeller cut into the top of the vehicle and a worker was fatally injured. The nose of the plane was then decorated with the image of a "teacup", along with the existing painted bombs and swastikas indicating missions flown and enemy planes destroyed.

During wartime, a more macabre humor prevails and is generally accepted.

Upon our arrival in Britain, June 1943, our unit was assigned to an 8th Air Force base near the town of Shipdham, in Norfolk, the home of the 44th Bomb Group, one of the first heavy bombardment groups sent to England in 1942.

Our first assigned overseas duty was on the evening after our arrival when the squadron's corporals and sergeants were to guard planes dispersed around the perimeter of the airfield. Two of us found ourselves transported by jeep at dusk, to where a huge bomber lurked in the gloom. We each took a five-hour guard duty, interrupted only by the surprise return of the jeep, bringing wonderfully welcome sandwiches and coffee.

For that short, near summer solstice night of not more than five hours actual darkness, time crept slowly along in the cold. We had no idea where we were.

When dawn arrived we found the object of our guard duty to be a battle-scarred veteran B-24, *Suzy Q*, with its share of recorded bombing missions and combat successes.

(Nearly two months later, we learned that *Suzy Q* was the ship, which carried Col. Leon Johnson and his crew through the hell of Ploesti, the flight which brought him and other leaders the Congressional Medal of Honor. Shortly after that devastating oil field raid, the faithful old Liberator, with a new crew, was lost over Italy.)

As I recall, our second duty, for three days, was on the base tennis courts, digging weeds and related work. For this, we came across the Atlantic?

Well, who can assess the value of such duty on the total war effort?

(None of our bunch ever got to play tennis there, anyway).

Girls, yes, surely a significant component of the remembrances of most veterans! And Britain was full of girls, all types, just like home.

The attractiveness of those girls of the fabled "sceptered isle" was attested to by the many war brides who followed their soldier, airman, sailor sweethearts to a new home in America at the war's end.

How was I to guess, that two years later I would be sending an engagement ring back across the sea to England?

What about the girls we left behind at home? Well there are those old sayings: "Distance lends enchantment; Out of sight, out of mind; Absence makes the heart grow fonder (or is it "makes the heart go wander?)."

Yes, I had left a girl behind; not at home but deep in the heart of Texas. The pangs of absent love due to distance burned brightly for some time, but like a flower, at last they faded away. (I heard later that she married a second lieutenant!).

England's countryside was beautiful to see whether on foot or bicycle or by any other conveyance. In the early summer brilliant red poppies dotted many fields and the green hedgerows and narrow lanes were not anything like home.

During most of the three months I was at Shipdham, the 44th was gone from England, as we would learn later, to North Africa for the daring low level attack on the Ploesti oil complex and other Mediterranean targets.

The Shipdham Airfield was not deserted, however. Royal Air Force Stirling bombers and other aircraft used the base for practice landings (and takeoffs) often at night. And from the tower we saw many types of planes for the first time.

Except for the "tennis court" work, it was more than a week before any of us were assigned for training. I was lucky; a clerical slot at the Control Tower, "Flying Control" per the Royal Air Force terminology. Some of our squadron were being sent to a new base soon to be operational. Others and I would follow, but we didn't know when.

While at Shipdham, three of us somehow managed to be housed in a small hut, rather than in one of the barracks buildings. We three managed some sense of independence, not experienced before or after.

Soon we found a farmhouse not far from the base where we could actually buy fresh milk and real eggs! (Where was all the reported rationing?) We found a means to boil the eggs in the little hut we were occupying; also we didn't miss hitting the mess hall and also more eats at the base Snack Bar. (Doesn't an army travel on its stomach?)

Obviously, all those airfields scattered over eastern England were formerly peaceful farmlands. Between the runways at Wendling one local farmer tended to his sugarbeet crop while bombers were landing very close by. Perhaps that duck pond near the Control Tower and its fowl, belonged to him.

I got my first 12-hour pass nearly two weeks after arrival. A truck ride and a bus took a buddy and me to Norwich. Had supper, saw a show, couldn't make connections with any of the fair sex. Got lodging at a large Red Cross Club on the grounds of the 900 year-old Norwich Cathedral, a huge and magnificent structure.

Ann Hathaway's cottage, Stratford-on-Avon

Next morning, we walked around in Norwich sightseeing and taking the first pictures with my faithful Argus camera. Among the city's sights were plentiful bomb ruins. A train-ride and a long walk took us back to the air base. Met two pretty Royal Air Force girls on the train, but unable to make a date for another meeting. Better luck next time?

Two days later, we checked out bicycles from Ordnance, pedaled to the town of Thuxton, put the bikes on a train and on to Norwich and the Red Cross Club. We found a dance in progress but when a British lass told my pal that "she didn't like Yanks," that spoiled the fun.

On our next foray into town we blundered into a "social" where most of the men were Canadian. When I asked one girl if she would like to dance, she told me she'd prefer to dance with her girlfriend!

Market scene, Norwich

CHAPTER 2

A month after reaching Shipdham, my luck changed, almost for a lifetime. At the Sampson dance hall in Norwich, a buddy and I met two very attractive Womens Auxiliary Air Force girls, danced with them and we all spent the evening together, even escorting the girls to their "liberty bus." My charming new acquaintance was from Cardiff, Wales, Myfanwy "Van" Williams.

Two days later I wrote to her and received an immediate reply. So, on the August Bank Holiday, we again met the girls. Dinner, a movie, a stroll around the Norwich Castle grounds. They were staying at the YWCA so we saw them the next morning for breakfast.

Three days later, another date. This time, Myfanwy and I went boating on the river and then another movie and the next day's breakfast. I was finding her a delightful companion, even with my thoughts mostly focused on Texas.

On our next date Van and I saw a rodeo put on by American ranchers and cowboys now in the Army, quite a sight for English eyes! I had just gotten my sergeant's stripes and Van immediately noticed. The next morning, Sunday, we went to a church service at Norwich Cathedral, far more ritualistic than my Methodist background but the Cathedral was very beautiful.

On our next meeting, Van was dressed in civvies, not in uniform and looking wonderful. She had just received her first promotion!

Our time at the Control Tower kept us busy and provided the necessary training

Myfanwy Williams in "civvies."

we required. Two unexpected events brought the war to our very doorstep. Let me quote from my diary for July 1943:

"Two Stirlings arrived to shoot landings. One had engine trouble so only one flew. Just before 0400, Direction Finding called, saying a ship wanted to land. Just before the Stirling moved onto the main runway, Whoosh! Down came an RAF Halifax bomber for a crash landing through a fence. It burst into flames. Returning from a raid on Germany it was hit by flak and bullets, top gunner killed; four men bailed out near the field. Pilot brought her down without landing gear, flaps, only three engines and bomb bay open.

"Sparks sure flew along the runway. The New Zealander sergeant pilot came up to the control tower.

I recall him sitting down in the big chair, seeming less nervous than our tower crew and he asked, "How about a cup of tea, mates?"

Again from my diary for August, 1943: "Two RAF Stirlings came down to fly during the night. Just before 2230, Operations plugged the tower into an air raid broadcast, which came from Norwich.

"Operations gave a plot on an unidentified plane south of us. Two minutes later, Wham! Wham! Wham!

"Three bombs were dropped along our main runway. Sure shook the tower. I hit the light switch being closest to it. Our blackout curtain partly open. Men downstairs said they dove for the bomb shelter!

"Five minutes later the Royal Observer Corps an-

Control Tower, Wendling, 392nd Bomb Group.

nounced 'bombs in the Shipdham area.' One Stirling was on the ground, the other in the air with lights on and the field flare path was lit.

"The Jerry (reportedly a JU-88) had caught us with our pants down, cut his motor and dove in with navigation lights on, then gunned it. (We later heard that it had been shot down by an RAF night fighter).

"Supposedly, one of our anti-aircraft gun crews cut loose with a few shots at the RAF Stirling. Jerry had also dropped four loads of anti-personnel bombs, which kept exploding along the perimeter strip and aircraft dispersal around the other Stirling.

"Airfield closed until all bombs were removed. Next day, RAF demolition squad detonated 37 'butterfly' anti-personnel bombs."

In late August, 1943 the remaining B-24s of the 44th Bomb Group arrived from Africa, the battle scarred veterans of the Ploesti mission.

The group had been gone from Shipdham for two months. Other missions included targets at Vienna, Austria. Reportedly, the surviving crews were to be headed back to the States, heroes all.

One evening at Shipdham, a "Quiz Show" was held in the Aero Club and the Red Cross girl, Helen, with the ravishing figure, was Master of Ceremonies.

I was one of the contestants from our squadron pitted against three others from the chemical outfit. I missed one-third of two questions in the five rounds but our team won. Our prize was a carton of chewing gum. Lots of fun.

My Argus camera, which I had brought from Texas on my first furlough home, had survived the voyage in one of my over-stuffed barracks bags. And for the next two years it was a constant companion.

While at Midland, some now forgotten enlisted acquaintance had given me a large bulk roll of "Super XX" black and white film. (Color slide film was not so common then). I never did ask where the film came from. And that source provided many of the pictures, which accompany this wandering story and prompted many of these memories.

Myfanwy Williams and Al Enlow

Wall mural - former flying Officers Mess Hall, Wendling, summer 2001

Al Enlow and Myfanwy Williams,
Norwich, England

CHAPTER 3

The expected transfer from Shipdham to the new base was on September 12, leaving some friends behind but rejoining others.

Eleven of us boarded trucks with our overloaded barracks bags, for our permanent station at Wendling, now the home of the newly arrived 392nd Bomb Group. The next day, nine of us reported to Flying Control and were immediately set to work putting in posts for a rail fence!

However, the following day found us actually beginning our duties at the Control Tower.

After two days at Wendling, several of us were allowed to move to a barracks near the Control Tower. All crews were in training as were we. One day, the rudders had been switched on two of the new Liberators. Up in the tower, we couldn't figure how one supposedly grounded B-24 was taking off and another could land that we thought had not taken off?

The B-24 Liberators assigned to the 392nd were the new "H" model, the first to be equipped with power gun turrets in the nose, tail and belly. Look out, Luftwaffe!

It was reported that an English language radio broadcast heard from Germany had given a "welcome to the new B-24-H model Liberators at Wendling, England" and that "Goering's yellow-nosed fighters would be waiting for them." How did the enemy know all this?

After a double date Myfanwy and I shared with one of her RAF friends and a buddy of mine, he and I stayed in the annex of the Red Cross Club in Norwich. We had retired when other GIs came in. One of them somehow dropped a cigarette butt on another man's pants.

Suddenly my pal woke up when he smelled smoke, jumped up and put out the blaze on the unlucky guy's pants. We left early in the morning to meet the girls for breakfast, never learning how he made out without a full complement of trousers, a real case of hot pants.

For one date with Myfanwy, I got off the train in Norwich and discovered I had left my billfold back in the barracks. I only had a few pieces of change in my pocket, enough to pay for a bed at the Red Cross Club and one last shilling for a phone call to a buddy at the base.

But the operator cut me off before the call was completed. So I met Van without a pence in my pants.

I had to borrow a pound from Van so we two could go to the cinema for the delightful spoof on British military pomposity, *The Life and Death of Col. Blimp.*

Van's gracious loan was matched by the sweetness of the goodnight kiss as she left for camp. I had money left for a late snack at the Bishop's Palace Red Cross Club and for my return train fare the next morning.

A week later and with a 48-hour pass in my pocket as well as sufficient British currency, I was fully prepared for the delightful two-day date with my girl in RAF blue. But, when we met she was in civilian garb. Wow! A wonderful time together, including an afternoon boating on the river, relaxing along the banks with never a thought about Texas.

On one of our dates Van and I visited the 900 year-old Norwich Castle. We toured the battlements; a great view of the city from atop the old walls after climbing a steep, narrow and winding stairway.

In the old dungeon some of the instruments of torture and chains for the prisoners were seen. The castle had been surrounded by a moat in the Middle Ages, now gone. We were told that a French King (one of the Louies) once captured the castle from England's King John.

On September 14, 1943 the official ceremony of turning over the air base to American command took place in front of the Control Tower, including two honor guards and many officers.

The British flag was lowered and the Stars and Stripes was raised over Station 118, now officially the home of the 392nd Heavy Bombardment Group of the 2nd Air Division of the 8th Air Force of the United States Army Air Corps.

Another section of that previously peaceful East Anglian farmland had become an active part of the great battlefront.

A few days before, those initial cross-country training flights were over and the first of so many of the mission take-offs into the "wild blue" (more often gray) had begun.

One after another, 30 seconds apart, those heavily-laden, dark painted Liberators lifted from the Wendling runway bound for Hitler's Fortress Europe, their deadly cargo to be delivered through the skill, courage and determination of each and every crew.

On the first day of October 1943, a co-worker and I were walking back from supper when we passed a first lieutenant on an angle walkway without saluting. He gave us a first class "chewing out" for our omission in military courtesy. That was my first such being called down for failure to salute an officer since joining the Army!

Two days later, four of us from Flying Control got official permission as "passengers" on an old B-24 from Shipdham, for a flight to Landford Lodge in Northern Ireland. But the adventure was called off due to bad weather. Then we learned that the pilot for that flight would have been the lieutenant we didn't salute!

Bomb ruins at a Norwich Church

Later, I could have gone along on a similar flight to that Northern Ireland destination but my buddies (?) forgot to tell me ahead of time.

That first week of October, the third combat mission for the 392nd resulted in the first casualties on an otherwise reportedly successful foray to the Frijian Islands.

Three planes and crews were lost; two returned to the base with rudders partially shot off; one B-24 landed with bomb bay doors open; another ship had the nose turret shot away.

Thus, the reality of war contradicted the otherwise quiet of the East Anglian countryside as did the roar of the mighty engines each time the heavily loaded bombers departed from the Wendling Field as they did for a total of 285 missions September 1943 to April 1945.

Van had been home on leave, so 20 days after our previous date I met her London train at Norwich. It was great to see her! She had brought a sponge cake and cookies her mother had made for us. We sat on a park bench and munched all of the goodies and enjoyed being together.

It was at our next meeting, more than two weeks later, that Van told me of her pending transfer to an RAF base near Bath! (Closer to her home at Cardiff but a long way from East Anglia).

At 0100, the morning of Nov. 7, 1943 the tower phone rang. It was Van to report she was to leave the next morning for Bath. When I came off duty at 0700, I found our first sergeant and was able to talk him into letting me have a 24-hour pass.

Then I phoned Van and she, also, was permitted to get off duty so we could meet in Norwich. It was a Sunday morning so there would be no available train or bus into town until the afternoon.

Let me again quote from my diary: "I walked a couple of miles down the road, caught a ride to Dereham, walked about two miles down the Norwich road, got a truck ride for a few more miles, walked some more, caught another truck nearly to town, then got a ride in a Jeep the rest of the way.

"Was to meet Van at 1300 and I made it on the nose. Tired from all that walking but the autumn countryside was lovely. Scattered rain through the day. Van and I had a nice dinner at the Curate House Restaurant. Strolled about town most of the day talking and laughing. Saw a Hugh Herbert movie. Van leaves for Bath tomorrow, she had to go back on the 2200 bus. A few kisses before she left. Will miss her."

What my diary doesn't reveal, but is still in my memory, that night was one of the most romantic of my younger life. (No other adjective could be more suitable).

Instead of the usual farewell when the soldier is leaving and the girl is staying behind, my RAF girl was going from the bus station and I was the one remaining!

It was a cool autumn night with a full moon (or nearly full). The final moment in my arms, the farewell kiss, who could forget such a moment?

Although it took some time for me to recognize the change in the direction of my affections, that was undoubtedly the night Myfanwy won my heart.

Looking through my 1943 diary for the last half of that year and recalling my first meeting with Myfanwy in late July and her departure from East Anglia in early November, I now wonder why it took me so long to focus on England and lose track of Texas?

It wasn't "love at first sight" with Van, or me. But I do remember that at least with our second meeting, there was a mutual attraction and enjoyment in each other's company. And our first kisses were very natural and genuine.

There was never any awkwardness. Anyone seeing us together from the beginning might have thought we'd been together for a long time. Whatever we did or wherever we went on those early occasions (as well as later on) were mutually delightful. Even though I continued for awhile to correspond with the girl back in the Lone Star State, I always eagerly looked forward to the next date with the delightful girl in Royal Air Force blue.

Later notations from the diary: "Van is a lovely armful of charms" and still later: "she is so nice in my arms." And, "Van and I have a grand time together, what a wonderful girl she is."

Looking at the photographs I took of Myfanwy with my ever-present camera, in only two is Van not smiling her wonderful smile. How could anyone have resisted such a lovely smile? Obviously I couldn't.

I have oft pondered "what might have been" had Van remained nearby and had not been sent so far away that we could not meet as often as before. Even so, as will be related later, she became my fiancee when the time came to set sail for home.

When I first met Van she was working in Operations at a Royal Air Force combat airdrome. She did some airplane plotting and later, radar work.

Before becoming a WAAF she did nursing work following her schooling. Apparently her military career had begun in mid-1942.

At many, if not all permanent stations, the staff often entertained children from the surrounding areas, especially at holiday times like Christmas. And shortly before Myfanwy was transferred, she invited me to join a group from her Royal Air Force station who were entertaining some little orphan children (perhaps some who were separated by the war from their parents). I believe we took the youngsters to a theater and then for goodies. Everyone had fun, the RAF hosts, hostesses, the children and also me.

Myfanwy and I were looking forward to meeting in London in mid-March 1944 and a hometown buddy was hoping to join us. But disaster! And I was the cause and also the victim.

A surprise inspection of our carbine guns resulted in about a dozen of us being restricted to the air base for a whole week, the week my pass had been approved! Supposedly, our guns weren't clean as expected. But none of us had touched them since we were in overseas training in Florida nearly a year earlier. And the guns were never fired again.

Had Van still been close by, the canceled leave wouldn't have seemed such a calamity. However, coordinating our leave

Myfanwy Williams, October 1944

times so we could be together wasn't a simple task. Ah well, the course of true love is seldom smooth. So it has been said.

When others and I were restricted to the base because our carbines were "dirty" and I missed seeing Myfanwy in London, the current issue of *Stars and Stripes* included an astrology column (which I seldom read).

Here was their 'prediction' for my Sagittarius birth sign:

"An unexpected snag will throw current plans out of gear and cramp your style noticeably. Less free time and sterner discipline during the first half of the week. But the situation will ease up later."

How about that? So the joke was on me, but not very funny.

At that time, no one could have guessed that later in the Spring because of the D-Day invasion plans, all personnel were to be restricted to no more than 25 miles from our assigned bases for most of the summer months of 1944. And there were more than several times 25 miles separating Myfanwy and me. Who knows what might have happened to us, had that insurmountable restriction not been in effect!

I do not recall whether it was at Shipdham or Wendling, but one afternoon an older officer appeared at the Control Tower with several of the "top brass." His uniform jacket bore many ribbons and decorations, on both sides. We were told afterward that he was one of the American volunteers who flew with the famed Lafayette Flying Corps of the French Air Service in the first World War.

One unexpected visitor to Flying Control at Wendling, was an outstandingly beautiful girl in the uniform of a flight nurse, escorted by several beaming officers. I believe she was an invited passenger on several test or training flights thereafter.

And her lovely face was later seen on the cover of one of the early issues of *Air Force Magazine*.

One bright day as the returning planes appeared in the eastern sky, one pilot called the tower to report severe battle damage and loss of vital controls.

Col. Lorin Johnson took the radio microphone instructing the pilot to try to gain more altitude, then set the plane on a course toward the North Sea and give the order to bail out.

When the B-24 headed back over the field, ten white parachutes were seen, one by one, as if the crew had had such a training exercise. One chute seemed to be heading for the tower and the nearby duck pond as the occupant loudly yelled "Catch me! Catch me!"

He missed both tower and pond and the entire crew was safely home, their wounded Liberator fading out of sight on its final flight.

There was never a combat mission day when the Flying Control area was not attended by personnel from all areas to "sweat out" the return of the planes. The seeming more important or lengthy the mission, the more who crowded around the tower watching the sky for those tiny dots and counting, flight by flight, plane by plane, as they neared their final approach to the welcoming tarmac.

Inside the Control Tower and on its balcony, officers and enlisted men strained their eyes as did all those on the ground below. Our crash trucks and ambulances were on alert for a red flare indicating wounded aboard, requiring priority in landing.

Sweating Out the Mission at Wendling

And then the watchers could see some of that day's battle damage as, one by one, the big B-24s passed by on the runway or the perimeter strip.

Lt. Ford's bomber, which had been built at the huge Ford Willow Run plant, was named *Ford's Folly*. Upon his return from one mission he taxied the ship to the dispersal area in front of the Control Tower. A few moments later, up the tower steps, probably by two at a time, came the pilot.

No one could have appeared more excited than Lt. Ford. "Come see my plane, you have to see it!"

So, some of us did. And on the left side of the Liberator, behind the pilot's seat, was a very large hole, from cannon shot or flak, so very, very close to having been fatal to Ford and his crew.

In early December, 1943 Capt. Glettler of Flying Control okayed 48-hour passes for Leonard Brooks and I. I sent a wire to Myfanwy, asking her to meet us in London.

My supposedly Texan sweetheart might have then been appalled had she known how eagerly I was looking forward to that reunion!

Brooks and I hurriedly packed our bags. To East Dereham via a civilian truck. Took the 1600 hours train to King's Lynn and the 1730 train for London. We rode in a car without compartments; just table-like shelves between the seats.

The London train was an hour late in reaching the Liverpool Street Station. Van wasn't there so we took our first underground (subway) to Marble Arch and got lost in the blackout. Finally found the Red Cross Columbia Club where there was no room for us. Took a cab to the R.C. Mostyn Club, got in line for lodging which was in an annex a block away at Portman Square.

Brooks and I then made our way to the Victory Club and found the hoped for message from Van. She, too, was in London!

Sandwiches and coffee at the snack bar, a blackout walk near Marble Arch and to bed at 0300 hours.

Let me continue from my diary: "Up about 0800, breakfast at the Red Cross Club, bus to Sloan Square and on to the King George and Queen Elizabeth Club to meet Van at 0930. She looked as pretty as ever."

(No other trio of "tourists" could have been more excited or enthusiastic or have seen more of London's historic sights!)

Back to the diary: "Subway to Marble Arch, got mixed up and had to back track several Underground stops. A delicious meal at a Lyon's Corner House on Oxford Street. To Westminster Bridge on a bus via Piccadilly Circus. Walked past the Houses of Parliament with the famous Big Ben clock tower. Walked across Westminster Bridge over the Thames which was almost lost in the haze which hid most buildings from successful efforts at photography.

"Saw interior of St. Margaret's Church where the fashionable weddings are held. Then to the beautiful and famous old Westminster Abbey, built in the 11th century.

"Saw Poet's Corner and the graves or memorials of Lord Tennyson, Kipling, Samuel Johnson, Elizabeth Barrett Browning, Macauley and others. We were told that 14 kings and 14 queens are buried behind the high altar.

"The Abbey is full of memorial tablets, statues, etc. Altar is beautiful and the windows exquisite; some had been removed.

"Walked through Whitehall to Trafalgar Square with the famous tall Lord Nelson monument, then up the Strand. Streets and walks crowded and with all kinds of military uniforms.

"Our threesome had tea and cakes; then booked seats at the Victoria Palace Theater for 'The Love Racket' with well-known comedian, Arthur Askey, a good musical show. Excellent seats, sixth row from stage (17 shillings each). Show also included a lot of lovely girls.

"Subway back to Marble Arch to reserve lodging, got the last available beds at the Columbia. We three had a late dinner at the Corner House at closing time, fried SPAM! Then I escorted Van back to Sloan Square on the Underground. Some sweet kisses and back to the subway. Went past my station and just caught the last train back to Marble Arch.

"Brooks and I up at 0800, no mirror in wash room so I shaved 'blind.' Met Van at Corner House for breakfast. Walked down Oxford Street and a bit of shopping at Selfridges, a very large store.

"Underground to London Bridge Station. I nearly got us all lost in that part of the huge city. Walked across Tower Bridge, still too hazy for good picture taking. Fine lunch at Lake Restaurant on Tower Hill. Saw bomb ruins of old All Hallows Church which has Roman ruins beneath.

"One hour tour of the Tower of London, a history lesson come to life! The most interesting part of all our sightseeing.

"Our tour guide dressed in the old red and black garb of the ancient Tower soldiers. Saw Chapel of St. John-in-Chains where rest the bodies of many who were beheaded in the Tower. Also saw the famed Bloody Tower where the imprisoned were kept; the Cathedral Tower with the Norman Chapel of St. John and the large room exhibiting old armor, swords, etc.

Sgt. Al Enlow, Weston-Super-Mare

Traitor's Gate, Raleigh's walk, the Bell Tower, remains of an old Roman well, the Ditch or moat which was drained by the Duke of Wellington.

"The large ravens at the Tower are on the daily ration account of the garrison at three pence each! (It has been long rumored that if ever the ravens leave the Tower of London, that will signal the end of England!).

"The large tourist crowd that day at the Tower were almost all in uniform, both men and women.

"Back to Oxford Street Underground Station, kisses and a fond farewell to Van as she took subway to Paddington Station and the train back home. Van's mother had sent me a pack-

Myfanwy Williams, Bath, England

age, beautifully wrapped for Christmas, with a delicious cake and home made candies which Brooks and I readily devoured.

"Got seats in the last truck from King's Lynn to the base and back to the barracks at 2345."

Back to the old diary for December, 1943:

"Lights went out at the field for several hours, portable generator working at Control Tower. All quiet until about 0130 when all of our on-duty crew were jarred out of our seats by an explosion which shook the tower.

"Rushed out on the balcony, saw a B-24 in the 579th Squadron area, broken in the middle and ablaze. phoned for fire trucks and ambulance and aroused our crash crew (who must already have been so moved).

".50 caliber bullets, incendiaries and flares were exploding a ghastly display of 'fireworks.' A few minutes later a second bomb apparently exploded, again shaking the tower. Could see pieces of metal falling nearby. A gas truck was also ablaze, at first we thought it was another plane. A third explosion and shortly a fourth which scattered the fire.

"Lt. Kriesman and I were on the balcony, we both hit the floor! Never heard whether any ordnance or armament men were injured or not. The plane burned for about three hours.

"Our crash crew was right on the job and Capt. Glettler and Lt. Swift were also on the site. Both came back to the tower covered with extinguisher foam. Lt. Kriesman said the last bomb blew his hat off.

"Learned the next day that a second B-24 was also ruined by the blasts, only useful for 'graveyard' parts. Later on, one of the crash crew was awarded the Soldier's Medal for having hooked up a small tractor and pulled one Liberator out of danger."

Again from a 1943 diary entry:

"Our planes went on operational mission, we were told over northwest Germany. After supper, several of us walked out on the field to the controller's position near the runway to watch the late in the day return.

"First two planes landed with wounded aboard, 45 minutes after expected estimated time of arrival (ETA). Several rough landings. Suddenly, we saw a B-24 (from another group) on a very low approach, angled toward the runway and heading right for us! Did we scatter!

"The plane managed to hit the runway, nosed down and scraped to a halt at the intersection with the cross runway, nobody hurt. Rest of our group came down in moonlight. Two missing, reportedly from flak."

Touchdown at Wendling

Wending Air Base

CHAPTER 4

In mid-January 1944, Myfanwy and I were able to coordinate our leave times so that I could accept the invitation to visit her and her family in Cardiff, South Wales. Not only could I be with Van again, so soon after our London adventures, but have an unexpected opportunity to spend several days with a family in Great Britain.

Rather than quote from my rambling diary again, let me enter into this reminiscence a copy of my letter to my parents in Ohio, telling in detail of this most pleasant experience away from the air base, to wit.

Jan. 29, 1944: Saturday night, at tower
Dearest Mom & Dad:
Perhaps after a few night shifts, I will again be caught up on my letters. Received five more in today's mail call; two from y'all and one letter from a fellow who was among the 10 who left Midland almost a year ago. Tonight I want to tell y'all as much as possible about that furlough, if I can stay awake. We just had our evening tea, toast and cookie party and was it good! We're out of tea now. Could you send me some more?

Won't be long until Valentine's Day, will it? Did I tell y'all what I gave Van? One of the RAF lads who used to work with us in the tower had made a heartshaped pendant out of Plexiglas, with the RAF insignia from a blouse button set in it. He gave it to me, which was certainly nice and I got a lovely tiny gold chain for it. Will be something Van can wear when she dresses in civvies.

There is so much to tell about that "vacation" that I wonder if I won't forget many of the most interesting things and incidents. Will just leaf through the ol' diary and give a day by day account. Got a good start when our breakfast at the base included a fried fresh egg, pancakes and an orange!

Went by train to London, changed stations via subway, then got the late train for Cardiff. Traveling at night on English trains is not much fun, as stations are not called out in the usual manner of American trains and it is often difficult to know where in heck you are. I dropped off to sleep once and when I awoke and glanced at my watch, it was 3 o'clock in the morning and I was sure scared that I'd gone way past my stop. But the jolly train was just late, as is the wartime habit of English railroads. Reached Cardiff about an hour later and Van and two of her sisters were waiting for me at the station, a most welcome sight! After walking to her home through the blackout we had a snack to eat and I enjoyed a delicious fresh fried egg and hot tea.

The room I had at Van's was very nice and was the bed ever soft and comfortable! I slept in silk pajamas that I suppose were her brother's and also had a hot water bottle to keep my feet warm! How's that for luxury? Oh boy!

Van woke me about 11 and brought me a cup of tea to drink before I got out of bed. Ah, the Army was never like that, huh? Met most of Van's family that day and what a nice family she has, quite a large one, too. They all certainly treated me wonderfully and I really was made to feel at home there. One of her married sisters was staying there and she has the loveliest little girl, about 4-1/2, an adorable youngster named Ann. Van's father is retired and I don't really know just what his former occupation was. One sister, Evelin manages a large downtown shoe store and her brother is in the Army, stationed in southern England. Another brother was killed while on flying duty with the RAF, about two years ago.

Cardiff is a clean looking city. Van lives in Roath Park, a nice section within a block of a large and very beautiful park, which has gardens, tennis courts, walks and lawns and a sizable lake. Their house is in the middle of the block, one of a long row of nearly identical appearing houses, which are all joined together, as it seems most homes are built here in England. But it sure puzzled me as to how Van could tell which front door to enter when we came home in the very dark blackout without a flashlight! The house was very nice inside, though of course heated by a coal fireplace in each room instead of central heating, which is almost taken for granted in the States.

Van and I walked downtown and the next day she showed me some of the sights. Actually, the business districts of the larger English cities and towns differ only slightly from the average American city. We saw the university, War Memorial, City Hall and the Museum, the latter two being fine buildings of white stone. All these were in one area, with wide avenues and well kept parkways. The Cardiff Castle is nearby which is still occupied by Lord and Lady somebody and not open to sightseeing. But it really looks as one imagines a castle should be with battlements, walls, towers and a real moat. Spent about an hour in the fine museum and saw the bird room, zoology, geology and botanical rooms and also some ancient Welsh relics. Suppose one could almost spend a furlough in the museum alone.

When Van and I had had our afternoon tea (quite a nice English custom) we went to the cinema and saw a double feature. The first was a Jack Benny comedy, the second the Technicolor picture, *My Friend Flicka*, a story of a boy and a horse with some beautiful western scenery. Then we rode home in the tram, had

Myfanwy "Van" Williams

some supper, sat by the fireplace for a while before bedtime.

Saturday was a rainy and unpleasant day. Again, Van brought me a cup of tea to drink in bed. That morning she and I went for a walk through the park, but it was too damp to take many pictures. Went downtown again after dinner and did more walking and sightseeing. Managed to book some good seats for a stage play or rather an operetta, *Old Chelsea,* at the Prince of Wales Theater. We enjoyed the show, which had some lovely stage settings and good music. Back home, where we two "kids" washed the supper dishes.

Evelin told me about some of the bombing raids they'd gone through. Their lovely church was completely destroyed and her sister Connie's house was also nearly demolished. They all had spent many nights in the not-too-comfortable air raid shelters. If some of the American civilians could see the results of the enemy's bombs on English homes and buildings, perhaps they would realize how fortunate America has been to escape such terror and would gripe less about living costs and lack of silk hose and gasoline, etc.

On Sunday morning Van, her sister Olwen and I went to church in the small building which the parish is using since the Germans bombed the church. It was a Church of England service, even more formal than the one at the Norwich Cathedral. The next time we two go to church together, I want to take in a Methodist service, as the Anglican Church is too ritualistic to suit me. Van, three of her sisters, little Ann and I took a walk before dinner. The sun was shining nicely when we started, but we were caught in a hail shower, which was real fun to little Ann as she darted out in it and was having the time of her young life trying to catch the small hailstones!

Sunday afternoon tea was really a meal, with plenty of tea and all sorts of delicious pastries, pies, tarts and such. There was quite a house-full, as besides various sisters and all, Van's girlfriend came and one of Van's sisters brought an American tech sergeant, who is at a nearby camp (the lucky stiff). Aside from washing the dishes, most of the afternoon and evening was rather quiet.

Before going to bed, Van and I pressed some of our clothes and shined our shoes. I also had a nice hot tub bath, the first time I've had other than a shower bath since I was home last year! I almost fell asleep in the tub!

Van and I got up earlier than usual the next morning and had swell-tasting soft-boiled eggs for breakfast, another treat. It was raining again, or rather yet. Her sister Eve saw us off on the train for Bristol, where we had lunch and then took a bus down to Weston-Super-Mare, a fine resort city on the sea. We found accommodations for the night, Van at a private boarding home and I got a bed at the servicemen's hotel.

To our pleasant surprise, the sun suddenly came out at just the moment we wanted to begin our sightseeing and stayed out the rest of the afternoon. Weston would surely be a beautiful town in the summer, but is pleasant even at this season. The ocean-front is lined with hotels and there are long parkways and walks, theaters and dance places built out over the water, a very modern swimming pool, outdoor concert stages, etc. There are rocky terraces and gardens along one section of the beach. Hope all the pictures we took while at Weston turn out good. We were forced to take shelter in the Winter Gardens pavilion for a few minutes during a sudden rain flurry.

When it grew dark, we found ourselves a restaurant and almost fainted on the spot from shock when we were told the menu could either be steak or lamb chops, instead of the usually offered fish, chips, sausage, etc. Van and I ordered steak and it was quite good, though a bit tough. We saw a movie afterwards, *Flesh and Fantasy,* a very strange but interesting movie about dreams, etc. There was a terrifically strong wind blowing when we came out of the cinema, and we had to hold tight to our hats, as well as each other. After we sat on a bench in a sheltered spot for a while, we headed for our lodgings and sleep.

I've always referred to my lovely WAAF girlfriend as Van, but have I ever told y'all her real first name, which is Welsh; Myfanwy. It's pronounced as if the first "y" were an "a" and the "f" a "v." What a grand girl she is . Hope I can see Van again in March when she gets her next few day's leave.

It was still windy the next morning. We wandered about the shops and down by the beach again. After lunch, we took the bus to Bristol, which appears to be rather a dreary city and then another bus to Bath. The sunshine almost deserted us for the rest of the day, worse luck. Strolled about, had another nice supper and then Van had to return to camp. Isn't it too bad the war has to interfere with our private fun?

I stayed at the American Red Cross Club in Bath, which is located on top of what must be the highest hill in a hilly city. Gosh, what a climb! Must be at least a mile and it seems to be almost straight up when a guy is tired and lugging a pack full of stuff. Y'all should have seen all the junk I stuffed into my bag for this furlough. The only thing I forgot to take was shaving soap. While climbing the hill to the club after Van left, my hat blew off and I had to scramble down the street about a block before I caught up with it.

I'd sent a wire to Jimmy, a home town pal, but there was no word from him at the club, so I planned on spending Wednesday looking for him. First, I looked around inside the 15th century Bath Abbey, which has some beautiful and highly colored windows. Wish I could really describe how lovely they are and the appearance of the old church, whose walls are covered with various memorials, as are most of England's old churches and cathedrals.

Then I took the first bus to (censored) arriving at that small town in the rain, which I was becoming very used to. That entire section of England, from Weston to (censored) is lovely country with rolling hills, winding roads and old farms and villages with old walls and buildings. I'd like to tour that section in a private car in more pleasant weather.

When I reached (censored) I began to inquire of every GI that I met as to where Jimmy's particular section of his division was located. Finally, one fellow told me they were just at one edge of the town, so I started walking. When nearly there, I passed another soldier and I happened to ask him more directions and if he knew a guy from Ohio named Sayers. Believe it or not, but this particular fellow was carrying a note Jim had written to me and he was going to leave it at the servicemen's canteen in town! The fates were being kind to me, I guess. He had just received my wire that morning.

When I found where Jim was located, it was chow time, so I went into their mess hall, saw him chewing a piece of GI meat. I walked over and tapped him on the shoulder and did it surprise him! He's located at a very nice spot and is conveniently near the town. Jim couldn't get off that afternoon, so I waited until he finished work, then we took a bus into Bath.

Gosh, was it great seeing him again. We just talked and talked all the time we were together, about our various experiences and also of the wonderful fun we used to have back home. It was very dark and though I couldn't purposely locate the restaurant where Van and I had dined the previous night, we found it much by accident after stumbling about in the blackout. Jim also stayed at the Red Cross Club and we sat in the lounge until after midnight just talking and laughing.

The next morning, Van came in from camp on the early bus and Jim and I met her. We three had breakfast together, then went to see the famous ruins of the old Roman baths, which date back to 54 AD, and took a lot of pictures. The hot springs have been famous for centuries and it was certainly interesting to see the old Roman ruins of what used to be elaborate baths. We also went to the Pump Room and drank some of the hot water from the King's Spring. Wish we'd had more opportunity to look around Bath and the surrounding country, as it is full of interesting sights.

After we saw Jim off on the bus back to his camp, Van and I had a snack at a cafe, then a sweet kiss before she took her bus and I got my train for London. The rest of the day was rather uneventful. When I reached London, I was surprised to find I had three minutes to make an earlier train than I'd expected, so I went dashing madly across the station with my bag swinging on my hip and made the train with a minute to spare. Spent that night at the Red Cross in Norwich, got up early and came on to the base in time to go on duty yesterday.

Boy, but I did have a lot of fun and wonderful time on this furlough, folks. Hope I haven't forgotten very many interesting things to tell you all. What fun Van and I had together and I was so glad I was able to spend that time with Jim. If I hadn't received his letter before I left, how sorry I would have felt on returning and learning I'd just missed seeing him. Am hoping he and I can meet in London about the middle of February, if we can arrange our passes accordingly.

Guess this is about enough for one letter, or the censor will be on my neck! Will try to answer all your accumulated letters tomorrow night. What do you all think of the news regarding the Jap treatment of Allied prisoners of war? Those dirty (censored) will surely pay dearly for that and soon, too. When this war is over, it will take an archeologist to find the remains of Tokyo!

With all my love,

CHAPTER 5

Army food, chow, was it as bad as often griped about? At the two English bases where I was stationed, maybe some "never had it so good." Day in day out, we were well fed with more variety than we might have expected considering wartime shortages and having most, if not all supplies shipped in to that "tight little island." It just seemed natural to gripe about something and the everyday chow was an obvious target!

Probably the two most complained about foods were the powdered eggs and "SPAM." An unknown creator of the war's shortest "poem" was quoted in the *Stars & Stripes* newspaper: "SPAM? Damn!"

Often the penalty of being among the last to arrive at the mess hall for lunch or supper was SPAM in place of the expected but all-eaten-up entree. I was never certain that what we were served was the same product as that sold at home but I'm probably prejudiced by faulty memory.

Breakfast usually alternated between hot cakes and powdered eggs but occasionally the latter was on hand two days in a row, to our consternation and we'd be outguessed on going or not going for that early meal.

Maybe the Army cooks never had a good recipe to suit that substitute for fresh eggs. A little restaurant I found in historic Bath offered outstandingly delicious omelets. I could hardly believe my taste buds when I learned that they were actually made from that oft-avoided powdered variety.

Those maligned Army cooks always did rise to the occasion for Thanksgiving and Christmas with a holiday meal

Cpl. Al Enlow

to rival those back home and usually, at a permanent station, all you could eat. From my notes, Christmas dinner in 1943 consisted of the following: punch, soup, salad, roast turkey and dressing, baked ham, gravy, mashed potatoes, peas, corn, rolls, two kinds of pie, cookies, cake and candy! And the tables actually had cloths, candles and little Xmas trees. (And, no SPAM).

Our second Thanksgiving Day in Britain (1944) furnished another excellent holiday meal. But, as never before or after, something went wrong at our non-flying enlisted men's mess hall.

As usual, some officers were guests at our noontime feast. And what followed apparently did not occur at the other mess areas.

In the late evening - disaster, "the runs" – not for a few but everybody! During much if not all of the night, barracks' room and latrine doors slammed open and shut and sounds of human distress were everywhere.

Coming from the latrine about dawn I met one of my good friends, almost falling off his bicycle and then weakly heading toward the latrine door.

In passing, I asked where he'd been. His hurried reply was "Trying to get to the base hospital, my third try."

Some couldn't find an empty latrine stall so had to use a ditch or hedgerow or elsewhere. Never did really hear how the officers fared.

Fish and chips! The British know the secrets of that famous combination. It was seldom difficult in town to find a little stand or shop selling those tasty morsels.

Paper wrappings or bags were nearly non-existent because of the war. Civilians had to bring newspaper to carry away their fish and chips but military personnel were served by the vendors. A little newsprint never hurt anybody or affected the taste!

Two of us were "victims" of a hungry and enterprising mouse who had chewed his way into our barracks bags at Thanksgiving time and found the cakes and cookies we'd received from home.

So, we plotted "revenge". We put water in an empty can, took three bricks, a mirror for a "gangplank" and some cheese on a wire in the middle of the can and set the proposed trap at bedtime.

Next morning there was the drowned mouse! We never had to try the trap idea again and no one beat a path to our Wendling barracks door to see the "better mouse trap!"

At Shipdham, my buddies and I had been frequent visitors and patrons at the large Red Cross Aero Club; snack bar, reading areas, games, etc. So, upon arrival at the new Wendling base, that welcome facility was missing.

However, two days before Christmas (1943) the Wendling Aero Club was opened; even better than at Shipdham! And so beautifully decorated for the holiday! The two charming girls in charge were from Ohio and Texas. From the Buckeye state, Birdie Schmidt. Some months later, a newly delivered B-24 Liberator was christened and painted in her honor.

With that year's excellent mid-day Christmas dinner, no evening meal was served at the Mess Hall.

But at the Aero Club "plenty of eats" and seemingly, everyone on the base was there! And the goodies were "on the house."

At the gift drawing for 80 packages from America. I actually won one! A box from a lady in New Mexico with candy, cookies, a book and other gifts.

There was no lack of entertainment at the two air bases where I was stationed. For the early days at Wendling, before a full projection facility was completed, the movies were shown on a 16mm projector. On one occasion, we were witness to an obviously old British "mystery" film. Before the final scenes, the film broke and the show couldn't be completed.

No loss, all agreed. In my next letter home, I wrote that the plot in the never finished story was as clear as "a chemical warfare lecture."

So, who do you suppose was the officer then assigned to censorship duty? Yes, the lieutenant or captain who lectured on "chemical warfare."

I was called into the squadron commander's office and lectured on my written comment as upsetting to "morale on the home front."

When the full screen movie facility was completed at Wendling, we saw first run movies regularly and usually the movie was shown on two consecutive evenings. Reportedly, US military installations received some new pictures before they were released to the public. This supposedly included such films as *Going My Way* and *For Whom the Bell Tolls*.

I was very impressed with the latter and my duty schedule allowed me to view it again the second night.

Live entertainments were also frequent. USO shows and British performances afforded opportunities to see movie stars and other excellent entertainers. Among the former were James Cagney, Stubby Kaye, Adolph Monjou and undoubtedly the highlight, the Glenn Miller Air Force Band at Wendling on August 25, 1944.

Because of dismal weather, the band had to perform inside one of the large airplane hangers instead of outside. Obviously, a standing room attendance, some hanging onto vertical wall supports! An unforgettable event and if you weren't a Glenn Miller fan before, you were then. That exciting one-hour concert included some old Miller favorites, with Ray McKinley and others from the former big bands.

Another outstanding entertainment for personnel of the Second Air Division was held in the Theater Royale in Norwich, a high-class burlesque show presented by performers from London's famous Windmill Theater, the theater that never closed even during the Blitz. The large crowd included officers and enlisted personnel, female as well as male and also some Britishers.

Several of the lovely showgirls posed with bare breasts and some GIs flashed lights at them, which brought a manager on stage to complain. No complaints from the audience!

Some months later, Myfanwy and I saw the show at the Windmill in London.

A group of previously professional entertainers then in the British army, "The Norfolk Turkeys," were at our base at least on two occasions and probably the best of all the variety shows we saw.

An American USO group, "USA Calling," included the "Three Nonchalants," acrobatic comedians with an unusual slapstick routine; also three gorgeous American girls, a singer, an acrobatic dancer and a comic stooge. The Master of Ceremonies began with "Ladies, Gentlemen and Second Lieutenants."

One of the staged entertainments called "Skirts" had an opening scene in a Nissen hut with the top sergeant trying to get the guys out of bed, they were garbed in "Long Johns." Hadn't realized just how comical that could be.

In another skit called "Passing the Buck" a general was kicking a major who jabbed a captain in the rear with a bayonet who then hit the lieutenant with a mallet; the Louie then knifing the sergeant and the latter squirting the private. The ol' Army game!

And another hilarious skit, "Three-Day Pass" showed three ways to be turned down for such a request. About that same time, the usual three-day pass was no longer to be given, only one for 48 hours! (Nice while it lasted).

Another show at Wendling was "Liberator Cavalcade" with Yank talent, including WACs from the Second Air Division. One GI put on a clever "strip tease," which had many in the audience convinced he was a "she."

The deadly toll of the air war was never forgotten even with the interludes of mirth and laughter on stage or screen. Among my early notes is this entry, "a Liberator from Hardwick landed here with the top turret gunner frozen to death." And diary entries: "one plane did not return," "one ship from each squadron was lost," etc. And each Liberator with 10 brave men aboard.

Al Enlow at Westminster, London

In re-reading my old letters sent home, I realize how few times my writings were censored. In correspondence from former friends also in the service, some had been heavily censored.

Such scanning of mail was obviously important but I wasn't the only GI who resented having my intimate expressions and thoughts always perused by a stranger. For a change, we GIs ought to have been able to read some officer's mail! Wouldn't that have been revealing!

One funny wintertime incident is worthy of being noted herein. On a morning when the roads on the base were slick with frost, a lieutenant on a brand new bicycle skidded off the roadway and into a water hole supposedly about 18 feet deep. The officer was fished out of the water but the bike went to the bottom.

Some time later, the air base fire crew needed to test some sort of new pump so they pumped the water from that same hole.

While that was being done a chap from my squadron passed by and said the crew might find a good bicycle at the bottom as the lost bike supposedly had never been recovered.

When all the water was pumped out, the missing bike was pulled from the mud. But nothing was left except the frame!

Obviously, someone had managed to hook the bicycle from the bottom, then taken the wheels, seat, chain, etc. and thrown the frame back in the hole.

As the early weeks of 1944 passed, those awaited letters from Texas soon indicated that I would not be returning to Midland. And as that realization grew, so did my thoughts of the charming WAAF way across the British Isle and not so accessible as when she was also in East Anglia.

CHAPTER 6

On a visit to London when Van was unable to obtain leave to join me, I went on a walking tour led by a very articulate and knowledgeable former British army major. Here is one of his stories regarding the seeming fact that many native Londoners often don't know a great deal about their own city.

It seems a workman was on a ladder painting Marlborough House when a lady came along and asked him where St. James Palace was located. The Palace is only a few yards from where the painter was laboring but he replied, "Blimey, lydy 'ow should o'i know? O'im a blinkin' Londoner!"

While walking through Trafalgar Square with the tall column honoring Admiral Nelson, our British tour guide pointed out four huge lanterns taken from Nelson's flagship. He remarked that the British never threw anything away; they always kept everything on display somewhere!

At the beginning of March 1944 the new concrete barracks were ready, so another move to far more comfortable quarters with 16 double bunk beds. All the Flying Control personnel were now together and with linoleum on the floor instead of bare concrete.

Charing Cross, The Strand, London

I had again chosen the bottom bunk. Seems I can always roll out of the sack far easier being on the bottom tier.

But the adjoining latrine unit wasn't complete, including the showers. By summer?

During one of the winter cold spells, we returned from lunch to discover that the Supply Room lads had stripped one blanket from each bunk to have them cleaned. (?) Br-r-r. The Army way?

At about the same time, I received a letter from Myfanwy in Devonshire saying that due to the cold weather, she had been huddling over the stove wearing her great coat and gloves and at night, burrowing under four blankets! And without much hot water and no hot water bottle for her feet.

In another letter from Van she wrote that she had been staring at the lovely moon and hating to see it going to waste. (Me, too!)

In one diary entry I noted having had my monthly hair cut. Our barber by night was an electrician by day. If I recall, he was of Swedish descent – the land of the Northern Lights?

We had an unofficial "sack time contest" among our barracks mates, but, believe it or not, I wasn't even in the running! One of our buddies was sometimes referred to as "Horizontal." But I did my share of sleeping and warned my parents by letter that when I was discharged and returned home, I would need a very loud alarm clock and even an automatic upsetting bed.

An amusing incident reported in one of Van's letters concerned a dance held in honor of the Fifth Anniversary of the Women's Auxiliary Air Force, the "WAAF." The girl at their RAF station who had been there the longest was chosen to cut the big cake. But when the time came, she was not to be found, having left the station without a pass.

And about that same time, Van and a girl friend had gone to Bath for the day and bought some fresh cherries en route to the cinema. Then, they became almost too ill from eating too many cherries to make the cinema.

On one icy day my bicycle slipped on a sharp corner and I ended up on my rear without the bike. Later that same day, one of the squadron commanders was approaching me on the wrong side of the little road. To avoid him, I again went flying off my bike, again on my backside but this time with more pain.

That same winter, a newly arrived staff officer had promoted an official order that officers were always to be saluted even when riding bicycles. That proved disastrous when saluting two approaching officers whom I knew from the Control Tower visitors. Again a slippery surface, but they did return my salute while laughing as I went head over teacup again.

The questionable regulation on saluting was negated shortly afterward when one high-ranking officer fell from his bike and broke a leg (or arm) returning a salute!

Four of us en route to Norwich had hitched a ride in a British "cracker box" type of command car. The driver stalled it going up a little hill. So, we passengers had to get out and push the bloody vehicle to the top so it could be started going down the slope.

Another "transportation tale" involves my undue delay in buying a new tire and tube for my second-hand bicycle.

Having once more noticed a lack of sufficient air in one tire, I set to work with my meager supply of tools and found a tiny hole in the tube.

Having patched (supposedly) the leak and inflated the tube, I was in the midst of replacing the wheel on the cycle when "Bang!" the blasted thing blew out and almost scared several of my barracks mates out of their sacks.

What's that about "a stitch in time?"

Coming off duty about 7 o'clock on a dark, dismal winter morning, my buddy, Mac, and I passed up the not too tasty powdered egg breakfast and plunged into our respective sacks.

Apparently we had just fallen asleep when the assigned Charge of Quarters entered the barracks to awaken any oversleeping, duty scheduled GIs.

He mistakenly and unceremoniously shook my just retired colleague into befuddled wakefulness.

Enlow with his trusty tire pump

49

Mac jumped up in total confusion ran, down the dark aisle and jerked me out of bed, shouting, "Wake up, Wake up! We're late! We'll be court-martialed, c'mon! Hurry."

Evidently, I had not fallen into such a deep slumber; but, it took me more than a few minutes to convince Mac that neither our military careers nor our freedom were threatened and that we rightly belonged back in our waiting bunks.

In October 1944 I was allowed enough leave to again visit Myfanwy in Cardiff. As before, her mother and others of her family made me feel at home and very welcome.

When Van and I left Cardiff we also visited with her sister Gwen and her family in Paignton, Devon, close to the more widely known sea coast city of Torquay.

One afternoon, Van, her niece Ann, her nephew John and I went strolling along the sea coast roadway. I was of course in uniform; Van looking lovely in more attractive civilian garb. As we four walked along, all hand in hand, obviously appearing like a family, we became aware of the many very curious inquiring looks from people as we passed by.

We could guess at their mental calculations: "The Americans have only been here for about two years, the children are several years older. How? When? Where?"

A view of Teignmouth, Devon, with Myfanwy and her sister Gwen Mortimore

CHAPTER 7

On a clear and otherwise uneventful night at the control tower we became aware of an increasingly loud throbbing noise. Going outside onto the balcony, we realized what we heard and briefly saw, at not a great altitude, must be one of the German V-1 "buzz bombs" which appeared to be on a course parallel with the main runway.

The invading flying bomb (called "doodle bomb" by the British) which had been launched by the Germans from across the Channel quickly disappeared out of sight and sound, but seemingly not toward London, the usual target area for these frightening Nazi weapons.

A few weeks later, it was my turn to do the all night duty as Charge of Quarters at the Squadron Orderly Room. Just after midnight, I again heard that same throbbing sound, so I hurried outside the hut to listen and almost immediately there was a very loud "bang" somewhere not far away.

Suddenly, I was thrown back against the doorway, obviously from the blast as the missile hit and exploded.

The next day, I heard that the site of the V-1 "landing" had been located; apparently the only casualty had been a small animal, possibly an unlucky rabbit!

On a day when some flying was going on at Wendling but no combat mission, the commanding officers were in the tower. As a B-24 was poised for takeoff, one of the officers was heard to say that the pilot was going to be one of the best in the group.

But, as the Liberator neared the end of the runway, it was not becoming airborne and ended up in a field with reportedly only minor damage.

However, that young lieutenant did become one of the leading pilots and earned promotions and became a staff officer.

As the air war progressed it had been determined that eliminating the dark war paint on our bombers would increase their speed and bomb load capacity.

When the first of the bright silvery B-24s was delivered to the 392nd, it shone like a diamond on a jeweler's cloth.

I believe it was on its first mission when someone in the Control Tower remarked on the contrast with the older, dark appearing planes as the group took off for their German target.

That afternoon, all but one plane returned to the Wendling tarmac. Yes, the new bright B-24 was missing; a possible victim of anti-aircraft fire. Fate or ill luck?

And supposedly, crews were somewhat reluctant to fly in the next silvery Lib until several more were delivered to our base.

On New Year's Eve when 1944 turned into the last year of the long war, I was on duty at the Control Tower. As the midnight hour approached we heard what sounded like shots or bombs.

Stepping out onto the tower balcony we could see in several directions toward other AAF and RAF bases, flares of both red and green heading skyward. Happy New Year, of course!

Not to be outdone by our military neighbors, we grabbed flare pistols and joined the "fireworks" celebration!

Outside the tower, our crash crew was not going to be left out, so they took the mortar unit and launched a bright parachute flare into the dark sky with its loud roar.

Immediately the tower phone rang and one of our Flying Control officers, I believe it was Capt. Glettler, asked what was going on and "he didn't want to hear another" mortar launched flare go upward.

Immediately, however, flare number two was sent skyward with the accompanying boom! I believe that concluded our own noisy celebration. I can't remember whether the captain came to the tower in person, or not.

One afternoon as our daytime tower shift was going off duty one of the pilots asked if any of us wanted to go along on a short flight to another 2nd Division base (it was either Hardwick or Hethel). Several of us then checked out the required gear and climbed aboard along with a skeleton aircrew.

After landing, we passengers just lounged on the grass near the plane until the officers returned. One of their errands may have included refreshment at the Officers Club bar.

When the Liberator leveled out for the landing at home it must have dropped about 50 feet. We were sitting on the deck in the waist area and when the wheels made a noisy contact with the runway, all of us were launched off our butts.

On another occasion, a couple of us from Flying Control went along with Capt. Miller for a short flight, perhaps to test new engines as we did not land anywhere else.

We were allowed to stand somewhere at the rear of the cockpit area as I remember looking forward and seeing the water as the big plane was put into a dive over the Wash area on the East Anglian coast.

My slight tendency toward motion sickness resulted in having to make use of my fatigue cap when we landed; I then threw the soiled cap into some tall grass near the dispersal area.

The next day I reported to the Supply Room that somehow, I had lost my fatigue cap and could I please be issued a replacement.

As mentioned earlier, military duty schedules for both Myfanwy and me kept us apart too often and for much too long following her departure from East Anglia.

Many of my subsequent solo wanderings and "sight-seeings" were of short duration but helped by the Flying Control rotating duty hours. This allowed a frequent day and a half off duty. Combined with an occasional short pass, I managed to visit such destinations as Canterbury, Cambridge, Stratford-on-Avon, Warwick, London of course and always with the faithful Argus camera.

On two occasions, I got to the ancient and fascinating city of Canterbury with its famous bright Cathedral and earlier Abbey ruins. During my first visit, along with an also camera toting RAF corporal, we met the man responsible for the maintenance safety of the Cathedral.

He escorted us up to the top of the Cathedral tower and showed us the huge vertical walk-around-inside wooden wheel used to lower or raise the large, heavy bell.

We learned that within a week or so he was to be honored in London by the King for his heroic efforts during one of the German fire bombings, which threatened the Cathedral.

At the time of my second visit, I was at Canterbury a day or so before Easter Sunday and heard some of the rehearsal of the Cathedral boys' choir – wonderful voices and singing!

My only visit to Cambridge (except for passing through en route to or from London) was to meet a former barracks mate from the Midland, TX Air Base.

It was an unusually beautiful afternoon weather wise and we strolled around the university grounds, talking and exchanging memories of Texas and subsequent experiences. I only took a few photos since I was to stay there overnight while my friend returned to his station.

But the next day – FOG! Not a little but a lot! So the remaining half day of my pass was a photographic disaster and I never got back for another trip.

On another dull, but not totally impossible day for photography, I was at Warwick Castle. That famous site looked as a medieval castle should to American eyes.

There were few other visitors, and I was able to closely approach one of the castle grounds strutting peacocks. As if that particular bird knew he was the sole center of attraction, he spread his spectacular tail and slowly turned around for his portrait, much as a human model might pose for a photo.

On one of my train trips to London I had boarded a car with the double seat compartments the width of the car, no front to back (or back to front) aisle-way. Halfway along on the journey I felt the urgent need to seek a toilet facility.

At the next station stop I quickly disembarked and found the men's room along the platform. I wasn't able to re-board the same rail car (where I had left my meager luggage) so I hopped aboard the nearest car and rode there until the succeeding stop.

Al Enlow inside Flying Control, Wendling

Unlike most times when many military personnel were aboard, I had originally been seated with only civilian fellow passengers.

In re-boarding the original car I was aware of the obvious amused looks on others' faces, knowing full well why I had been missing from my seat since the previous stop.

Once I went into the large Selfridge's Department Store in London to purchase a greeting card (probably for someone's birthday) and another now forgotten item usually associated with a store's stationery offerings.

While paying for my small purchase I asked the very attractive young lady at the counter about the other hoped for product.

Her quick reply, "Don't you know there's a war on, Yank?" My only answer had to be, "Yes, ma'am. That's why I'm here."

Toward the end of an all night double shift at the tower, instead of my expected telephone answer "Flying Control, Sgt. Enlow," I said, "Flying Enlow Sgt. Control."

At the other end of the line I heard Col. Gilbert's amused response "How's that again, sergeant?"

On another early morning, after an all night shift, I was at the large blackboard printing the names of the pilots and their plane numbers and letters for the coming mission.

Col. Lorin Johnson had come up to the tower and was seated in the large lounge chair, watching me.

In an obvious teasing manner, he commented, "Is that the best you can do, sergeant?"

My reply, thoughtlessly, "Yes, sir. At this time of night."

(I was very glad that the colonel apparently considered the source and said nothing more).

Flying Control often had visitors and on one occasion the Group's Chief Flight Surgeon was there while very little activity was occurring around the airfield.

I had crumpled a large piece of paper and instead of putting it into the wastebasket I had picked up a ruler and was tossing the wad in the air and attempting to hit it with the ruler (a la baseball style).

After several futile swings and misses the major said, loudly and laughingly, "That's okay, sergeant. You can stop now. I'll make a note of it for your medical and health record!"

One of the members of the Wendling military police unit was an always-cheerful chap with an obvious prodigious ap-

petite. Anyone meeting him coming from the Mess Hall and on inquiring about the day's menu, "How's the chow today?" would be answered by "Good! Good!"

I remember one holiday (Thanksgiving or Christmas) with its always-abundant menu when that young man went back for a complete re-supply of food. Amazing, but true.

Before the war, I was never much of a letter writer. That began to change during the year I was stationed at the Midland, TX Air Base. Then, for

Al Enlow

Al Enlow assessing the damage. *Al Enlow at Flying Control, Wendling*

the two years overseas at Shipdham and Wendling, my correspondence output reached its all-time zenith.

On many long night shifts at the Control Tower, when little or no flying activity was taking place, the Flying Control typewriter was worked overtime, often up to 50 letters each month, the V-Mail type.

And when I wasn't wearing out the Air Corps typewriter, I was probably reading, as were my comrades. On one long night shift I completely read *A Tree Grows in Brooklyn*. What a life!

Other recreational activities at Wendling included a men's Glee Club and a Photo Club but neither lasted as long as it might even considering the military needs.

The former was directed by a young pilot and our singing wasn't so bad. But the group broke up when the lieutenant was transferred, reportedly to the Supreme Headquarters flying staff.

The camera group included several officers and enlisted personnel. We were not only doing our own darkroom work but also some for others on the base. That activity, too, didn't continue as long as some wished it might.

C'est la guerre!

CHAPTER 8

May 8, 1945 V-E Day! (from a letter to home): "Three cheers, etc. Yep, this is the day we've been long praying for and looking forward to, the day the war in this part of the weary world is all over! No false alarms or premature celebration but the official and the real thing.

"And at one minute past midnight the Germans will have 'had it' and hopefully, for good. Yet, I don't feel any different than I did last week or last month and feel little but a sigh of relief that the conflict in Europe is ended for there's still a lot to be done before most of us can go back home to stay. That war with Japan may take quite a while to finish off.

"Even if I'm one of those who'll stay here and not go on to the Pacific, it'll still be many weeks before that happy day when we'll cram our junk into our worn-out barracks bags and sail for the USA.

"If I were in London or some other city or town on pass, then doubtless I'd be able to more readily get into the spirit of the V-E Day celebrations and merry-making. But here on the base, most of us hardly feel like any real hilarious goings-on.

"Probably the civilians both here and back in the States will do more celebrating than the service men and women and those who've never been overseas; they'll probably be in a more festive mood than we who are on foreign soil and have been for so long.

"Maybe this seems that I'm like a very wet blanket, but I can't honestly work up any gayety over the fact that only one-half of the world's ills are over with more fighting to be done as well as the tremendous task of rebuilding a peaceful and prosperous Europe and then a peaceful world.

"At the barracks this afternoon and evening we heard various radio programs in honor of the occasion including Pres. Truman's talk and those by Churchill and King George.

Myfanwy Williams in her civilian garb

A visiting B-24 at Wendling (from the 448th BG, Seething)

"One interesting BBC broadcast gave eye-witness accounts of the activities and crowds in London and other British cities including Bath and Cardiff. While the announcer was speaking from the Cardiff City Hall, in the background we could hear a Welsh choral group singing the 'Hallelujah Chorus' and I wondered if any of Van's folks were among the crowd.

("Now, Myfanwy and I may hopefully be able to plan our futures, together.)

"Of course the British people must be very thankful that the war with Germany is over, even more so than we Americans, as for nearly six crucial and trying years, this island was so very close to the war and was actually a battle-field, especially during the Battle of Britain and the V-1 and V-2 bombing.

"When I get home I'll tell you some of the things various people I've met here have told me about the days of the Blitz, as it would take too much time and space now.

"Lots of Yanks make rude and critical, unfriendly remarks about Britain and its people but they're often in

Bath, England

poor taste and biased, for every American ought to be grateful and appreciative of the fact that our homes weren't the targets for enemy bombs and rockets and our families didn't have to huddle uncomfortably and frightened in air-raid shelters, night after night.

"It's not that I'm pro-British in any way but I hate to hear some of my pals shooting off their mouths in an ignorant fashion about people and conditions in this country and I've been in many arguments in that way.

"This afternoon, there was a brief squadron meeting in the theater building. The Catholic chaplain gave a short prayer. After supper, several of us planned to go to the movie but it was canceled.

"Just after darkness fell there was over a half-hour's fireworks shooting on the field in front of the Control Tower with flares of all kinds shooting up as well as rockets. I was up on the tower roof with a good view of the event.

"Didn't have time to go to the Aero Club for free eats before going on duty at 2400 hours so our crew had steak sandwiches in the flare path tent which was better, anyway.

Al Enlow, "The Trolley Trip" May 1945

"The blackout restrictions have been lifted on the post and sitting up here in the tower for the first time with light streaming out from un-curtained windows makes us feel like goldfish in a bowl."

The second week in May, 1945 the 392nd and other bomb groups offered "Trolley Track Missions," sight-seeing flights across the English Channel to Germany's Rhine River areas to all non-flying personnel at the base.

These exciting opportunities have been described in detail in other books about the 392nd so I'll only relate my own re-membrances.

I went without any previous sack time following the night shift in Flying Control. After coming off duty at 0700, a buddy and I just had time to hit the mess hall and wash up before reporting to the "drying room" to pick up our parachutes and "Mae West" life jackets. Then we went to the "briefing room" where intelligence and operations officers explained some things about the coming trip.

We waited about an hour and a half before takeoff. Our Liberator had been christened *Hazee* with a luscious nude painted on the sides. Sixty of us from our outfit went on this

B-24 Hazee, Wendling

day's flight. Our plane had one of the group's best pilots at the controls. About three dozen B-24s were in our loose formation in three-plane elements.

Hazee was hostess to 11 of us passengers; I was one of the eight in the waist section, not as crowded as one would imagine.

Of course I had my camera but the day was hazy and cloudy so the photo results were satisfactory but not great.

We flew in a loose formation at an altitude of 1,000 feet or so and had a good eye's view of the former enemy countryside and the devastation from American and British bombing which was so vital to final victory.

We saw from the air, Cologne, Dusseldorf and other major target cities in Germany and Belgium, from a low, non-combat altitude, where our aircrews had contributed so much to the winning of the war.

Across Belgium, the Ardennes Forest, to the Rhine Valley; then back across Brussels and on to England. The flight took about six hours and 20 minutes and we must have flown about a thousand miles.

Near the Ardennes I began to feel a bit unsettled in the midsection partly due to the lack of sleep. One chap had become sick and I didn't want to follow suit. So I sat for awhile instead of standing at one of the waist windows, the gunners' position. I missed seeing some things, including the bombed Cathedral at Cologne.

The air was full of planes and we saw bombers of other groups near us. Our pilot said afterward that he would have circled several points of interest but didn't because of the other planes in the air.

As we crossed into Belgium the land was very flat with seemingly well kept farms. Like those in Britain, the farm buildings looked to be of stone and brick instead of wood as in much of the US. The landscape appeared quiet and peaceful and it was hard to realize that not long before, armies had marched and fought across that pleasant farmland and wooded areas.

Then we began to see bomb and shell craters, roofless buildings, zigzag trenches and the tracks of tanks and other vehicles. I also missed seeing the Remagen Bridge. Nearly every bridge over the Rhine had been destroyed by the Nazis, or us, but pontoon bridges were visible.

When we reached German territory the bombed and shelled structures increased. A casual glance at the cities we passed over showed how thoroughly our Allied planes had done their jobs.

Rail yards were especially hard hit and industrial areas seldom spared but we did see one large factory seeming entirely free from damage. We saw strafed trains and sunken barges. Many buildings had a large Red Cross on the roofs; really hospitals or German protection of vital points?

The Rhine valley looked very beautiful with rolling hills

Myfanwy Williams and Al Enlow, Roman baths, Bath 1944

and ridges which made the air currents rough, flying over them at low altitude. Several times we were actually below the level of high hills. Our planes did no "buzzing" as some other groups apparently did.

Dusseldorf in the Ruhr Valley had been badly battered with block by block of buildings entirely gutted.

It was startling to look out of the waist windows and see another Liberator almost wing tip to wing tip and we could almost tell if the other pilots had shaved recently! What cool and steady nerves it must have taken to fly a tight formation, hour by hour, on the actual bombing missions.

Having missed the mid-day meal we were really hungry when we returned to base, though we had been given small boxes of carbohydrate candy to fill the gap.

I had stood up to take a picture of the B-24 beside us when we got over the field at Wendling and our three-ship element suddenly peeled off for the landing approach. We weren't expecting that maneuver so soon and nearly all of us were thrown off balance. It was a good thing that the waist windows were closed or some of us might have gone sailing out.

Upon landing, it felt funny to walk again after so many hours in flight. We just had time to make the mess hall for supper. Then a hot shower to take away the stiffness and the tired feeling. I would have liked trying it again the next day but I was scheduled for duty.

I felt that experience made most of us ground personnel more fully aware of the dangers, the bravery, dedication and sacrifice of all our pilots and crews on all of those long and fateful missions against Hitler's legions.

Less than a week following the "trolley trip," a comrade and I took off on a furlough to Scotland and Northern Ireland. I can just imagine anyone reading this account must be wondering, why Scotland, etc.? Why not down to see my lovely Myfanwy Williams?

That had been my first hope but Van's duty schedule and leave availability made that a wish rather than a reality. She wouldn't then have been able to get off duty and away from her RAF station often enough for us to enjoy being together.

So that visit would hopefully (and did) follow shortly afterward.

Immediately upon my return to Wendling from that extensive and most interesting furlough, I had a half-hour phone conversation with Myfanwy who was then home on leave but ill from food poisoning. She did not feel able to make the long trip to meet me in Norfolk so I became determined to see her soon, somehow.

A couple of days later I got approval for time off from the tower and was granted a 24-hour pass to meet Van in London.

It had been four months since we had been together in Bath so even a few hours with her would be worth all the trouble and travel!

I caught a ride into Kings Lynn to catch the London train.

I met Van at a girls' service club. Then steaks at a small cafe and a musical comedy, "Something for the Boys" and sweating out a long queue for ice cream.

Van was to return to Cardiff on the midnight train, to conclude her leave. As I didn't have to be back at Wendling until midnight the next night, I decided to go to Cardiff with Van even though my pass was only for London.

Luckily, it was a Friday night and there was an extra and fast train to Cardiff, two hours less time than the "milk" trains! It was not the best time of night to travel but I didn't mind, with Van's head on my shoulder and my arms around her to keep her warm, of course.

We were able to get a taxi at the Cardiff station to take us to Shirley Road where her mother came down to greet us and fix us some fresh eggs which tasted wonderfully good.

She insisted that Van and I get a little sleep and I again could stretch out in a big, soft bed for the first time since my last visit.

When Van woke me about 8 o'clock I thought I was dreaming; seeing her lovely face. I wished she could greet me that way with such a smile, every day!

Shirley Road in Cardiff, South Wales (near Van's home)

After breakfast I was able to see Van's sisters, Connie and Evelin, and to meet Dorothy. So that left her brother Ken as the only one of her family I hadn't met. He was in Holland with the army and all were excited at his homecoming the next month. (What nice in-laws they'd be.)

How I hated the thought of leaving Cardiff and Van that day. There are occasions in the army life when going AWOL is tempting. But I wanted to keep the few stripes I had earned so I rejected that thought.

Myfanwy went downtown with me to get the return train, our not knowing when we'd meet again.

Some might think it foolish of me to travel that far for such a short visit but seeing Van again made it all worth while.

When I reached Kings Lynn I went to the Red Cross Club and realized that I had only enough money for my bus fare to the base and couldn't afford anything to eat at the snack bar. But Van's mother had given me some cookies and a bit of Van's birthday cake so I didn't starve.

CHAPTER 9

The 15 day post V-E Day furlough in mid-May 1945, to Scotland and on to Northern Ireland, was quite an adventure for Sgt. Buford and I. But I had wanted to go the other direction to be with Myfanwy. As noted earlier, her RAF duty schedule made that possibility an impossibility.

We began the trip by hitching a ride into Swaffham to catch a bus to King's Lynn and then the northbound train. The floor of the jeep we rode in was filled with five-gallon cans so our legs and feet were elevated awkwardly.

When we reached Swaffham, both of us found our legs quite numb. Thus, we fell out of the jeep, in full view of several local civilians.

The looks we were aware of reflected their imagined thoughts, "Look at those bloody Yanks, drunk at mid-day!"

When we reached Edinburgh late that evening, we were rewarded by witnessing the first turning on of the many lights at the huge Castle since the war had begun, nearly six years earlier. What a sight!

And another unforgettable sight that same week was seeing the royal family, King George, Queen Elizabeth and the two young princesses, passing by in a limousine with both sides of the main Edinburgh street lined with elbow to elbow soldiers.

Buford and I were among the on-lookers atop the portico of one of the large Edinburgh hotels. A real 'bird's eye view!"

Of course, we two GIs did all the usual sight seeing including Edinburgh Castle. Atop one old building was a "Camera Obscura" which had been in use for many decades, offering a no-lens unusual view of the city's skyline.

Our visits also included Linlithgow Palace, the home of the Stuarts, where the courtyard fountain flowed with wine, not water, at some of those long ago royal functions.

Leaving Edinburgh toward Glasgow, we found Loch Lomond and its "bonny banks" illuminated with perhaps the brightest, sunniest day of the two years in Britain.

Having met another GI, we three sergeants rented a row boat and went a-rowing on the Loch, finding a forlorn but romantic appearing ruin of an ancient castle along the shore.

After our water excursion, we came across a small café, with a sign advertising "Coffee" which we seemingly ignored by ordering tea!

We were then loudly and good naturedly scolded by the proprietor. "What's with you bloody Yanks, tea, instead of coffee?"

That delightful individual, a former BBC entertainer, and an expert in Britain's many dialects and accents, regaled us with wondrously humorous examples of those many interpretations of the English language. Blimey! (Oh, to have had a recording).

Then, on to the Irish portion of our trip. No inside seating on the crowded overnight ferry from Scotland in chilly weather. Upon our almost dawn arrival in Belfast, we found an American Red Cross Club offering both food and lodging.

For our first breakfast on the "emerald isle" we were offered poached eggs, as many as we wanted! What a treat after the scarcity of fresh eggs for so long at the Mess Hall. I believe we each had five eggs along with other enjoyable fare.

From the Club we joined several tours and excursions with both British and American uniformed visitors. A little train took one group of us to the northern coast to see the world renowned "Giant's Causeway," basalt formations looking hand made, not by nature. The only discomfort was the rainy weather but the unusual sight was worth the dampness.

Taking a regular bus, Buford and I headed south from Belfast one day for a visit to a particularly scenic part of the seacoast and mountains.

But the bus broke down, so we decided to take advantage of a very beautiful morning and began to walk toward the distant objective. Not long afterward, the supposedly crippled bus came along and the driver totally ignored our waving arms and disappeared into the distance.

It was a pleasant walk but we never did reach our intended destination.

On another damp day we decided to take in a movie. Waiting in line behind us were two girls with the obvious smiling Irish eyes, so we asked if they would join us. This they did and afterwards we four took in a visit to a pub for supper.

However, with Myfanwy almost always in my thoughts, that acquaintance was brief, though pleasant.

For both the week in Scotland and the following week in Northern Ireland, I recall that in each area, it took the entire week for us to be able to almost understand first the Scotch accents and then those of Ireland! The King's English certainly takes many forms.

Back across the Irish Sea and then the long train ride down to London for our final furlough day. The train was quite crowded; either stand or sit in the aisle on our packs.

Finally, nearing London, some passengers had alighted and we did find real seats.

In London, short of money but not unhappy, we met another GI from Wendling. I had been carrying an American two-dollar bill since Labor Day 1942. Then, to walk across the bridge from El Paso to Juarez, Mexico, we could only take American money in the two-dollar category.

I exchanged that bill for a half-pound British note so I could afford a small snack before boarding the train back to East Anglia and "home."

When the actual departure date from Wendling was announced, I rushed to find a pay phone beyond the airbase entrance, to call Myfanwy. We both obtained permission for a short leave, so we hurried via train to meet in London.

Some details of that last bitter-sweet time together are lost in the mist of memory, but sitting on a bench somewhere in one of London's many parks, in each others' arms, we made that mutual pledge of love there and then, not knowing where or when we would be re-united, or what the future might bring.

On Loch Lomond, Scotland

73

CHAPTER 10

That long awaited day to leave for home, mid-June 1945, arrived sooner than I had imagined. Climbing aboard the trucks for our departure from Wendling and looking back as the so-familiar Control Tower and other buildings faded from view was certainly a nostalgic moment.

On the troop train from King's Lynn en route to Scotland and the awaiting ship, we were fed K-Rations for the first and last time in my Army existence. The uncertainty involving the next duty assignment following the looked forward to 30 days R&R at home was to be expected. War in Europe was over; next stop, toward Japan?

I'm sure that my bulging barracks bags were not unusual after two years in one location. In boarding the *Queen Mary*, which seemingly towered over us, I stumbled along the gangplank and almost lost one bag overboard.

And, so, farewell to Great Britain. Would I ever be back? And when would I see Myfanwy again?

Our squadron was among the 15,000 who crowded the *Queen Mary* when she sailed from the Clydebank in Scotland.

Two years earlier, aboard the so much smaller *City of Antwerp*, Belgian registry, in what was reportedly the largest convoy to sail for Britain up to that time, few, if any of us became seasick.

But aboard the mighty *Queen,* when the ship reached the Irish Sea there was a "boat drill" and I was among the throng on an afterdeck. In the middle of the crowd and being of average height, the ship rolled so that I could see the water, first to port, then to starboard or vice versa.

Yes, most everyone became seasick, sooner if not much later. And as we headed for America, the open decks seemed far more welcome than the stuffy three-tier-bunk sleeping quarters.

As the first large "troop ship" to reach New York harbor, the *Queen Mary* was met by swarms of boats of all sizes and kinds, fire boats spouting water, ferries, yachts etc. What a reception!

Upon arrival at my Ohio home for the 30 days R&R, one of my first errands was to shop for an engagement ring. To avoid Myfanwy having to pay a heavy duty, I sent her ring in care of an old Midland friend still stationed in London and he conveyed it to Van.

She wrote that her RAF friends crowded around to see the ring and how, one night, the moonlight sparkled on the little diamond as she lay in her barracks bed.

Now that we were an ocean apart, those letters of uncertain arrival were our only contact.

Having met many of Van's family and with a sister who had married an American soldier, I know I would have been welcomed into their fold.

Myfanwy was a wonderful correspondent. From our earlier letters of friendship until our letters of love, only my mom and dad wrote more frequently while I was in Britain.

During the late summer of 1945, while I was in South Carolina awaiting the end of the war in the Pacific and a return to civilian life, Myfanwy and my mother corresponded. Mom wrote what a lovely girl I had found and how her letters from England reflected that loveliness.

Van had written to me immediately after receiving her engagement ring and said a girlfriend had acted as proxy for me, in absentia and had placed the ring on Van's finger. If only …

My dad wrote that Van and I should have married before my return to the States! (Had she not been sent so far from my own base, that could have occurred).

Earlier in February 1944, I had replied to a letter from home regarding "my getting into a romantic mix-up."

I had told Myfanwy about the alleged sweetheart back in Texas. Van then said she'd "never want to live anywhere but in England, so she wouldn't marry me even if I asked her!"

A year later, when I did ask her, Van's reply was definitely different!

The following reminiscence may not appear in my finished manuscript, nor in the hoped for published narrative. But it is an intense remembrance of that time just described and I want to put it in writing.

After leaving Van's family in Paignton, she and I went to the well-known seaside resort of Weston-Super-Mare for a day, or two, together. We found a small, resort type of hotel for our lodging. As we approached the reception desk, we were asked a supposedly obvious question, can't remember whether by a man or a woman.

Looking at us as a couple, a British girl and an American soldier, "Do you want one room or two?"

I am sure Myfanwy and I hesitated to reply, probably looking at each other questioningly. How soon we replied, I cannot recall, but we answered, "Two."

They were the last rooms available, across the hall from each other. Whether our last "Good night" and the accompanying kisses were in one of the rooms or in the hallway I do not remember.

I shall never know how that night is remembered, if ever, by Myfanwy. Now, two generations later, attitudes and social mores have changed. I'm sure that, back then, many of my comrades at Wendling might have said, if they had known, "You damn fool! You took separate rooms? Were you crazy?" Etc.

No, not crazy nor foolish, according to my own recollection. But, by that time, Van and I were really in love and aware of it. There had been many wonderful moments when she was in my arms, on a secluded park bench, in the Cathedral grounds, by moonlight or blackout, at other romantic sites. She was my girl and I loved her and respected her and had begun to think that Myfanwy might be the one who would be my girl forever.

Back to Weston-Super-Mare. Yes, it was very possible that we two could have chosen to ignore one room and be together as never before and sadly, as never after. Had we then shared that most intimate moment of love and how we would have remembered it years later, apart, we would never know.

Regret can take many forms. I hope with all my heart that my first true sweetheart did not regret our choice and has remembered me, if at all, as one who also preferred to wait 'til we might share a wedding night; true love, not just a brief wartime affair.

Rodgers and Hammerstein once said it in song, " ...now it's the thing with a ring for the payoff..."

EPILOGUE

After my discharge from the Army Air Corps at the end of October 1945, I enrolled in the University of Akron to pursue a degree in business administration. It should have been in history.

Looking back, I am certain that had I obtained my college degree before the war, Myfanwy and I would have married, possibly in late 1946, following her de-mob from the Royal Air Force, or in 1947. We corresponded regularly until late 1947 or early 1948. Then, Myfanwy returned the engagement ring, sending it to me by way of her sister, Connie, who was living in upstate New York.

It was not only the distance between Wales and Ohio but it was apparently well known that some British war brides were not happy residing in America and such marriages may have been discouraged by the military. I do not know whether or not her sister's experiences may have discouraged Van. Also, it might have been a very real financial struggle being married while I was pursuing my degree.

I do not really remember when, or why, we stopped writing to each other and there is the true regret.

Had we surmounted both time and distance, I would have placed that second ring on Myfanwy's finger. There will forever be a bit of my heart that belongs to her.

It has always been one of my major regrets that we two somehow failed to keep in touch as dear, dear friends.

When I became engaged early in 1951 to Marilyn-Jean Grotz, whom I met at the university, she accepted that same ring because she knew I had never seen it on Myfanwy's hand.

Rodgers and Hammerstein's musical *Me and Juliet* included a song entitled *Marriage Type Love*.

Thus, one small engagement ring has seemingly linked together the two unforgettable girls I have truly loved.

Looking back more than half a century, I realize how fortunate I was to be part of a Flying Control crew and to have observed some of the heroes of that second World War, commanders, pilots and others who often crowded the Control Tower.

The outstanding hero, of course was, Gen. Leon Johnson who had been given command of the 14th Combat Wing. He visited the tower on several occasions when I happened to be on duty. One afternoon he asked how we plotted an air raid warning when such a broadcast came from Ops in Norwich. When I finished he said, "Thank you, sergeant," the nonpareil officer and gentleman.

All these men were representatives of the finest that America could offer during that great human conflict. None should ever be forgotten.

At the end of December 1999, I had been working diligently at this writing project which I had begun several years earlier. My beloved Marilyn-Jean had passed away just nine months before. So, in remembering her and also recalling Myfanwy and with the nearly completed 20th century, there were many and very real tugs at my heartstrings.

I was certain that Marilyn would not disapprove of my re-calling the romance with Van if she were with me, just as I knew that she never forgot the Air Force boy she was once engaged to. He was lost during the Berlin Airlift.

C'est la Vie!

March 2000–

A collateral to these reminiscences is my current attempt to find Myfanwy Williams, if she is also still living. But, with so little information now available, that could be a formidable task.

Perhaps had I not lost my wife a year ago, that desire to search for my long ago wartime sweetheart wouldn't be so important.

Yet, Van is such a large part of my remembrances of those two years that I must continue the quest.

I have several organizations and friends in Britain who are also interested in locating her for me. And should any of these efforts be successful, I would want to send to Myfanwy some pages from this manuscript and some photos and renew our acquaintance, if possible.

Why I did not keep any of her wonderful letters and other helpful data, I cannot say. But, hope supposedly does spring eternal and if long ago love has any influence on Fate, who knows?

May 2000–

Myfanwy Williams has been found! A fervent wish has actually come true! Kismet?

In mid-April, a British friend sent a list of possible resources in eastern Wales. One name caught my eye, *The Village News*. I wrote to them, and the first week of May, a phone call and an E-mail message promised "some good news."

The next morning, at 4:00 a.m. Ohio time (9:00 a.m. in Britain), I phoned the paper and heard a remarkable account. *The Village News* is a monthly paper covering many small villages in Monmouthshire. The editor had sent a copy of my letter to a larger newspaper in Newport, Wales where one of Myfanwy's two remaining sisters (then nearly 90), an avid reader, saw the little article and telephoned Van.

Obviously surprised, after more than half a century, Myfanwy told the *Village News* that she would be pleased to hear from me.

In addition to Myfanwy's phone number and married name, I learned that she, too, was widowed and also has two grandchildren as I do.

Without hesitation, I placed a call to Van. But she had difficulty hearing my voice as a friend was in that very room repairing a large window, so with traffic noise, the other person standing near the phone and my apparent fast talking, Myfanwy felt her response hadn't been very warm.

May 2000

She phoned the editor and asked him to have me try again, which I did with little delay!

With that call and subsequent phone conversations across the sea and with immediate exchanges of letters, not only was our friendship renewed but also mutual feelings of affection.

In mid-June I will fly over to Cardiff, Wales for a three-week visit with my wartime sweetheart of so long ago.

Again, who knows?

September 2000–

We'll meet again ... Who of us serving in Britain during that distant wartime would ever forget that haunting song and the voice of Vera Lynn.

For me, those words have been so wonderfully apt, for Myfanwy Williams (Jenkins) and Al Enlow have, indeed, met again!

Fifty-five years since we were together. Yet, immediately upon my arrival in mid-June, it seemed almost as though we had never been apart.

My planned time to be with Myfanwy at her Cardiff home was three weeks. But, again, fate stepped in. Or, rather, I didn't step in.

While visiting in the East Devon seaside resort of Sidmouth, seeing that town's famed and extensive seaside gardens, I missed the step into the outdoor men's toilet (the *loo*) fell very heavily, smashing my right shoulder (and my camera) and blackened my eye!

The result, three months with Myfanwy while my medical and therapy treatments went on! What a lucky "break" to say the least!

That extended time allowed Van and I to re-kindle our mutual feelings for each other. Few summer times have been so delightful and rewarding.

How this story will end is uncertain at this writing. But it is certain that Myfanwy and I are again (or still?) in love. Perhaps her coming visit with me to coincide with my son's second marriage will determine our futures.

Reminiscence? Yes, indeed, with an unexpected but so welcome an encore.

A Sonnet for Myfanwy

How much do I miss you? Let me tell you the ways.
I miss your lovely smile; the same smile as long ago
Which helped to win my youthful heart those far off days.
I miss your dear, sweet nearness and your touch;
The glow that's in your eyes.
The warmth of your soft hands in mine.
Each day without you close seems always dull and drear.
When I awake and I'm alone, though sun may shine,
I know that day will endless seem with you not near.
Our love, ne'er forgot through passing years,
We've found again; rekindled now anew
And stronger than before.
Ne'er doubt you are missed day and night;
The latter when my arms long so to hold you close;
You whom I adore.
Sweetheart, should you miss me even half as I miss you,
Together, then, we must forever be. Our love is true.

A.R.E.
24 December 2000

Summer 2000

Photo Gallery

Al Enlow at Loch Lomond, Scotland

Wendling Control Tower, Flying Control

Throttling up a visiting B-17

P-47 at Wendling

British "Mosquito" at Wendling, in front of Control Tower

B-17 crash at Wendling (official photo)

RAF 'Boston - (B-25)

End of the Mission – B24's back at Wendling

B - 24 on final approach at Wendling, 392nd Bomb Group

River Avon, Stratford-on-Avon

Street scene, Stratford-on-Avon

Shakespeare memorial, Stratford-on-Avon

St. Paul's Cathedral, London 1943

Bath Abbey, Bath, England   *Somewhere in Norfolk*

Ancient Roman Baths, Bath, England

Sgt. Al Enlow

L.A.C.W. Myfanwy Williams (Van)
Royal Air Force 1944

Myfanwy Williams and Al Enlow,
Wales October 1944

Myfanwy Williams and Jimmy Sayers, Bath, England – 1944

Al Enlow at Wendling Flying Control

Al Enlow, somewhere in England

Myfanwy Williams in Devonshire October 1944

Al Enlow – Bath, England

Al Enlow at Flying Control, Wendling

Myfanwy Williams and her niece, Ann Marshall

Ann Marshall and John Mortimer, Van's niece and nephew, Torquay, Devonshire – October 1944

Ann Marshall and John Mortimer, Myfanwy's niece and nephew

Ann Marshall at Van's home, Cardiff

Myfanwy and an orphan friend

Sergeants Stanford, Blum, Horton, Enlow – Wendling

Myfanwy Williams and RAF comrades

Alvin Randall Enlow, Devonshire –
Autumn 2001

Myfanwy   Williams   Jenkins
Devonshire – Summer 2000

Myfanwy and Al at the 392nd Bomb Group Memorial, near Wendling
Field - Summer 2001

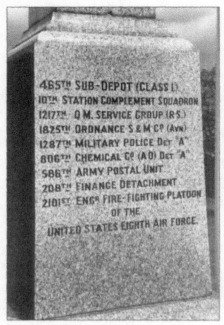

465ᵗʰ SUB-DEPOT (CLASS I)
10ᵗʰ STATION COMPLEMENT SQUADRON
1217ᵗʰ Q.M. SERVICE GROUP (R.S.)
1825ᵗʰ ORDNANCE S & M Cᵒ (AVN)
1287ᵗʰ MILITARY POLICE DET "A"
806ᵗʰ CHEMICAL Cᵒ (AO) DET "A"
586ᵗʰ ARMY POSTAL UNIT
208ᵗʰ FINANCE DETACHMENT
2101ˢᵗ ENGʳ FIRE-FIGHTING PLATOON
OF THE
UNITED STATES EIGHTH AIR FORCE.

392nd Memorial, Wendling   *392nd Memorial, Wendling*

392nd Memorial, Wendling

Printed in the USA
CPSIA information can be obtained
at www.ICGtesting.com
JSHW080004150824
68134JS00021B/2275